Original title:
Ripe with Desire

Copyright © 2025 Creative Arts Management OÜ
All rights reserved.

Author: Amelia Montgomery
ISBN HARDBACK: 978-1-80586-233-8
ISBN PAPERBACK: 978-1-80586-705-0

Passion's Bloom in Sunlight's Affair

In the garden of my dreams, I see,
Flowers giggle in the breeze,
Their petals dancing for me,
Waving like they're on a spree.

Bees buzzing like tiny drummers,
Pollinating with clumsy thunders,
Their buzz, a comedic croon,
As I chase them 'neath the moon.

The sun winks at my silly plight,
As I trip on roots in daylight,
With each stumble, joy takes flight,
A show of laughter, pure delight.

So let the blooms do their silly sway,
In this fanciful, vibrant play,
Where love's a joke that won't decay,
And sunshine laughs at the cabaret.

Corners of the Heart: Bursting with Hope

In the nooks where giggles grow,
Laughter's seeds begin to sow,
In the heart's corners, sweet and low,
Hope blooms bright, putting on a show.

Chocolate hearts and gummy bears,
Wobbling in their silly layers,
Sparkling eyes and playful stares,
Life's a circus without cares.

A wink, a nudge, a funny dance,
Love's a jester, not a chance,
With every giggle, I advance,
In puddles of joy, I prance.

So here's to hearts, all big and small,
With silly hopes holding them all,
In every tickle, we stand tall,
Bursting with joy, let's have a ball.

Craving in the Garden of Hopes

In the garden, tomatoes bounce,
They whisper secrets, kind of flounce.
Carrots giggle, a leafy mess,
While peas wear smiles, in bright finesse.

Sunflowers stretch, reach for the sky,
With dreams of bees that always fly.
Radishes hide, they laugh and jest,
In this patch, we find our zest.

The Allure of Sunkissed Wishes

Lemons twirl in a sunlit dance,
Chasing shadows, they take a chance.
Peaches blush with a cheeky grin,
While cherries conspire, plotting a win.

Grapes cluster close, with twinkling eyes,
Whispering stories in sugary guise.
They dream of juice in a fizzy spree,
A fruity party, just let it be!

Fevered Fruit of Twilight Nights

Under moonlight, apples gleam,
Their shiny skins a devilish dream.
Plums chuckle with a pop and splash,
While berries buzz, a wild dash.

Bananas split from laughing too hard,
In twilight games, they're the wild card.
Pineapples sway with a tropical cheer,
Their fruity antics draw us near.

Echoes of Avid Hearts

In the orchard, love is potent,
Peaches sway, their joy is molten.
Pears drum beats, a fruity tune,
While laughter echoes, under the moon.

Fruits unite in a grand parade,
Each one hoping to make the grade.
With every bite, they flirt and tease,
In this fruitopia, we find our peace.

Serenade of Sweet Temptation

In the kitchen, a pie lies waiting,
Fingers itching, the smell captivating.
Whipped cream dances, oh what a sight,
A spoon in hand feels just so right.

Chocolate drips like whispers from the pot,
Each bite laughing, a sweet, tasty knot.
Laughter bubbles, as crumbs take flight,
Dessert for dinner? That feels just right!

Encountering the Taste of Dreams

I dreamt a burger, golden and stacked,
With layers so tall, I barely tracked.
A pickle grin, it winked at me,
'Come savor my glory', it seemed to plea.

Fries lined up, all fresh and hot,
Chasing the sauce, oh what a plot!
Dancing with ketchup, a savory waltz,
In this calorie fest, I bear no faults!

The Garden of Unspoken Desires

In the fridge lurks a cheese that sings,
Wheels of delight, oh, the joy it brings.
With crackers nearby, a banquet's begun,
Nibbling in shadows, I'm having more fun.

Fruits lay scattered, a colorful mess,
Mangoed smiles and berry dress.
Each bite is a giggle, sweet and absurd,
In this garden of munch, I'm quite the bird!

Moonlit Fruits of Passion

Beneath the stars, the bananas sway,
Their peels whisper secrets, come out to play.
A cherry blush shines, and laughs in the night,
Sugary wishes, a fruity delight.

Pineapple pirouettes under the moon,
While oranges dance to a fragrant tune.
With laughter and juice, it's a zesty delight,
In this orchard of giggles, everything's right!

The Dance of Tantalizing Shadows

In the moonlight, shadows sway,
Chasing dreams that romp and play.
With a giggle and a tease,
They tickle hearts with playful ease.

A waltz beneath the starry skies,
Where laughter's echo never dies.
Twisting limbs in silly chore,
They whisper secrets, then explore.

Jumping high, they intertwine,
Spinning tales that taste like wine.
Around they whirl, a merry sight,
With shadows dancing, hearts feel light.

Abundant Whispers of the Soul

Whispers float on breezes bold,
Jokes exchanged, rich tales unfold.
A sprinkle here, a dash of glee,
What do they know? Just wait and see!

Sipping dreams from silly cups,
The soul sings sweetly, laughs it up.
With every nudge, every jest,
It's a banquet where quirks are blessed.

Winks exchanged, mischief in store,
Slicing air and dancing on floors.
Leave your worries by the door,
Here it's joy that we adore!

Strawberries at Dusk

With a splash of sweet and tart,
Strawberries tease, playing their part.
Sipping juice beneath the sun,
Laughter bubbles, oh what fun!

Red and juicy, a playful sight,
In the soft embrace of fading light.
Chasing flavors, who could resist?
Each bite a reminder to persist.

The fountain of youth in every taste,
Moments like these, we'll never waste.
Mischief drips from every leaf,
Joy and giggles—beyond belief!

The Lure of Juicy Enchantment

In a grove of dreams so bright,
Fruit dangles, a tempting sight.
Whispers dance on branches low,
Enticing hearts to join the show.

With a chuckle, grab a snack,
Sticky fingers—no looking back!
Giggling at a fruit parade,
Where laughter's hue will never fade.

Every bite a playful fling,
With each taste, the heart takes wing.
Joyous flavors intertwine,
In the realm where hopes align.

The Sweetness of Unspoken Dreams

In the kitchen, cupcakes thrill,
A sprinkle here, a frosted will.
But is it cake or just a dream?
With every bite, we start to scheme.

Chasing crumbs on a warm delight,
Imagining flavors, so sugary and bright.
Each bite whispers secrets in your ear,
Desserts become a source of cheer.

Chocolate fondue and laughter blend,
With every dip, we start to mend.
Sweet treats hold a charm divine,
Next time, I'll save you a slice of mine.

So let's indulge in our dessert schemes,
With spoonfuls of joy and frothy creams.
In this playful feast, we'll dance and hum,
In dreams of sweetness, we're never glum.

Nectar of Temptation

In a garden lush with juicy fruit,
You pick a peach, oh, what a hoot!
A bite reveals a juicy mess,
My sticky hands, oh I confess.

Watermelon smiles, seeds do fly,
As we laugh beneath the sky.
You say you'll share a half with me,
But save the chunk; it's my decree.

Lemonade sips in summer's heat,
With every gulp, we can't be beat.
Our glasses clink with fizzy flair,
In this sweet battle, who will declare?

So grab a mango, let's dance and twirl,
In our fruity world, we'll laugh and swirl.
With nectar sweet, temptation's true,
This fruity fun, I'll share with you.

Flesh of Forgotten Whispers

In the pantry, crumbs lay still,
Old cookies waiting for a thrill.
Beneath the dust, there's a tale,
Of snacks gone stale and cheese gone pale.

Leftover pizza, a time machine,
Takes us back to when we'd glean.
Whispers linger 'round each slice,
Should we savor or think twice?

Toasted bagels and jam galore,
The fridge is full; let's take some more.
Forgotten treats with tales to share,
Each bite is wrapped in daunting flair.

So let's feast on whispers of old,
In every flavor, our stories unfold.
These forgotten bites, my dear, are best,
In laughter finding a hidden quest.

Lush Fields of Intimacy

In fields of green where laughter roams,
We plant our dreams, build silly homes.
With daisies swapped for lemonade,
We're seeking secrets in the shade.

Picnic baskets spilled and wide,
Sandwiches dance, along with pride.
We roll in grass, oh what a sight,
Tangled up in joyful light.

Ants on a blanket, marching line,
Our lunch turned wild; it feels divine.
A toast to crumbs and friendship true,
In every bite, I'll savor you.

So laugh with me in this cozy spot,
With every sandwich, we won't get caught.
In fields of spirit—free and wild,
Together, we are nature's child.

Caress of Warm Breezes

In summer's grasp, we dance and sway,
With lemonade smiles, we giggle and play.
A wink, a nudge, oh what a tease,
Like ants on picnics, we can't find peace.

Pies on the windowsill, oh what a sight,
Giggling whispers under the moonlight.
Chasing ice cream trucks down the lane,
Our hearts racing faster than the train.

Banned from the cookie jar, what a shame,
But stealing a kiss? Well, who's to blame?
With silly hats and tickles so grand,
We laugh and tumble, hand in hand.

The warmth of the sun, mischief in tow,
Sweet summertime fun, oh how it does flow.
Like kids in a playground, carefree and bright,
We chase joy together, oh what a delight!

Velvet Night's Enchantment

Under moon's gaze, we wear silly hats,
Spinning like tops, running with cats.
A serenade sung, off-key and loud,
With laughter echoing, we draw a crowd.

Candlelit moments, shadows take flight,
Whispering secrets to the still night.
Using big words that we don't quite know,
Pretending to be wise in our silly show.

Snickers and giggles, they fill the air,
As we dance like ducks without a care.
With dreams on our sleeves and stars in our eyes,
We bubble and bounce, oh how time flies!

The velvet night wraps us snug and tight,
In this wacky space, everything feels right.
In our own little world, nothing's too strange,
Where laughter reigns, and hearts can exchange.

Elysian Fields of Affection

We roam through fields with daisy chains,
Giggling like cows with silly refrains.
Picking wildflowers, making them crowns,
In a world of our own, we dance like clowns.

Chasing butterflies, armed with a net,
Slipping on grass, damp socks are a threat.
Finding a puddle, oh what a blast,
Jumping right in, making memories that last.

Silly selfies with goofy grins,
Every click capturing our quirky wins.
We feign deep thoughts while snacking on fries,
Creating our tales with laughter and sighs.

In Elysian fields, we twirl and play,
In this joyous world, forever we'll stay.
With hearts as light as the clouds above,
We thrive here together, in mischief and love.

The Fragrance of Hidden Infatuation

In crowded rooms, we make a scene,
Sneaking sweet glances, as if on a screen.
With nervous chuckles and bumps in the night,
Crafting a chaos, oh what a delight!

Doodling hearts on napkins, so shy and meek,
Swapping sweet notes, with charms we sneak.
Like kids with a crush at the schoolyard swing,
Our worlds collide and butterflies cling.

With toothpaste kisses, we dare to combine,
Minty fresh moments, our secret design.
Caught in the whirl of endearing quirks,
In this playful maze, let passion lurk.

In the thrill of the chase, a funny charade,
With blushing smiles, our plans are laid.
In a dance of the heart, we both lay low,
Entwined like vines, in a silly tableau.

Blossoms of Quiet Desires

In gardens where secrets play,
The bees dance in a silly sway.
A sunflower winks at a bumble bee,
As though it knows their little spree.

Petals gossip under the moon,
With roses humming a cheeky tune.
Daisies giggle in the breeze,
While tulips tease with such great ease.

Each bud holds a smirk so sly,
Dreaming of rainbows in the sky.
A dandelion shouts, 'Look at me!'
As it twirls like it's carefree!

In the twilight, joy does bloom,
With scent of mischief in every room.
For nature's whispers, oh so bright,
Have us in stitches each delight.

The Taste of Starlit Hopes

Candy-coated dreams take flight,
Under stars that shine so bright.
A comet sneezes, what a sight!
Sprinkling wishes left and right.

Galaxies giggle with delight,
While moonbeams play hide and seek at night.
Light hearts bounce in rhythm and rhyme,
A cosmic dance, painless, sublime.

Shooting stars with silly trails,
Tell tales of love with goofy gales.
Constellations flick, a playful tease,
Even the planets join with ease.

So come sip this sparkling brew,
Of hopes and laughter, just for you.
With every sip, a giggle grows,
In a universe where joy overflows.

Tempting Glances in Twilight

In the dusk where laughter sings,
The fireflies wear their glowing rings.
A lone owl gives a wink and smirk,
While crickets join in their quirky work.

Moonlit paths and teasing glares,
The breeze carries fabled airs.
A shy fern blushes in the glow,
As shadows swirl in a gentle show.

Each rustle hides a playful jest,
While night unfolds its endless quest.
Whispers of wishes flutter near,
Bringing mischief wrapped in cheer.

So, let us dance beneath the skies,
Chasing giggles 'til we rise.
For every glance, a secret shared,
In twilight's charm, we are ensnared.

Whispers Amidst the Petals

In gardens where laughter blooms bright,
Petals whisper tales of delight.
With beetles boasting of their speed,
And butterflies teasing from their creed.

Blossoms sway with cheeky grace,
Each one trying to win a race.
Rosy cheeks all red with glee,
As morning dew spills like tea.

A daisy twirls, with flair so grand,
A clever smile, its upper hand.
While tulip giggles in the shade,
Creating mischief, bold and unafraid.

Here among the colored cheer,
Nature's humor, crystal clear.
In petals' laughter, joy ignites,
Whispers grow into endless sights.

Nectar's Call in Dusk's Embrace

In the garden of giggles, bees take flight,
Hoping for nectar under the moonlight.
With sugar-coated whispers in gentle air,
I chase shadows, but where's the flair?

Petals laugh softly, swaying in jest,
Bumblebees buzzing, they're on a quest.
I leap like a frog, but slip on a bloom,
The flowers all laugh while I trip and zoom.

The fireflies wink, with a flicker and tease,
They nudge and they natter among the tall trees.
A dandelion puffs, painting wishes on night,
But I just want candy and more silly bites!

Now twilight's a canvas, with giggles displayed,
As laughter paints colors, in wonderful shade.
With nectar dripping sweet, and giggles galore,
I dance through the garden, always wanting more!

The Scent of Longing Unfolded

There's a whiff of mischief, it's hanging about,
Like a sock in the dryer, there's humor, no doubt.
The roses are plotting in hues of delight,
While I'm munching on snacks in my pajamas tonight.

Lavender giggles, tickling my nose,
I'm a nectar-hungry bee, but my cake only grows.
A dash of honey laughter, what a strange brew,
I drizzle on muffins, and maybe my shoe!

Each scent in the breeze, has secrets to share,
With a wink and a grin, "Dance without care!"
The world's just a party, in folly we sway,
Where longing's a game, and we play all day.

So join in the laughter, let the petals swirl,
With each whiff of whimsy, we twirl and we whirl.
In this fragrant mischief, are dreams to unfold,
Let's brew up some giggles, and share a sweet gold!

Alluring Raindrops on Petal-Laden Paths

Pitter-patter laughter, as rain drops cascade,
Wet petals are sliding, in a playful charade.
I slip on a puddle, oh what a low dive,
Like a fish on land, but at least I'm alive!

The flowers are chuckling, with each little drip,
Dancing with raindrops, they're ready to flip.
I grab a big leaf, using it as a hat,
But now I'm a duckling, imagine that!

As thunder claps giggles, the sky starts to grin,
Bright lighting comes out, like a pizazz in the din.
Every splash tells a story of fun and delight,
As I twirl through the garden, all day and all night.

So bring on the raindrops, we'll splash and we'll sing,
With petals as pillows, and joy as the wing.
In this whimsical drizzle, our laughter will flow,
Like a river of joy, let the merriment grow!

Echoes of Sweet Anticipation

A giggle floats softly through the air,
As I dream of desserts, oh how they ensnare!
Chocolate fountains, with bubbles that tease,
I'm lost in a daydream, oh, take me please!

The cupcakes are dancing on the kitchen shelf,
With sprinkles a-swirling, they're winking, themselves.
Buttercream swirls like a merry-go-round,
While I swoon in delight, with pure treats abound.

A marshmallow whispers, 'Let's float on a cloud!'
With a sprinkle of giggles, we'll leap mighty proud.
The echoes of laughter, sweet love of a fork,
Join me in mischief, let's let dinner cork!

So gather the flavors, let's celebrate cheer,
With each sugary thrill, there's a story to hear.
In the kitchen of joy, where anticipation's a feast,
Life's sweeter than candy, where laughter won't cease!

Silken Caresses Under Moonlight

Frogs croak tunes, as lovers dance,
In soft shadows, hearts advance.
A picnic spread, wine flies away,
Cheese whispers secrets, oh what a day!

Whispers of silk in the night air,
Laughter erupts, do we even care?
A stolen kiss, a cheeky grin,
Under the stars, it's where we begin.

Starlit pranks ignite the fun,
Chasing each other, 'til day is done.
With giggles and snorts, we set the scene,
Love wrapped in jokes, oh isn't it keen!

So here we twirl, like leaves in the breeze,
With hugs and jests, life's little tease.
In moonlit glow, our spirits rise,
Silken caresses bring joy in disguise.

Enigmas Wrapped in Laughter

A puzzle solved by two intrigued,
Every word drips with mischief league.
Around the corner, a joke awaits,
Wrapped in giggles, love creates.

We spin tales with a wink and a nudge,
Like playful kittens, we never budge.
Try to keep straight faces, but why even try?
Our silly antics make the time fly.

Secrets like pies, we share them all,
Filling the air with our hearty call.
Every riddle, a playful dare,
Laughter our compass, a love affair.

So let's decode the mysteries laid,
In a world where chuckles won't ever fade.
In cozy corners, we'll rest our feet,
Enigmas unraveled, sweet and discreet.

Sweet Nectar of Serendipity

Two juicy fruits in a tangled vine,
Sipping sunshine, oh isn't it fine?
With every bite, we dance and sway,
Serendipity served on a silver tray.

Sticky fingers and sweet delight,
Whipped cream dreams in the warm twilight.
Sharing giggles over crumby treats,
Life's little wonders up and down the streets.

With every stumble, our joy just grows,
Tripping on laughter, nobody knows.
A dash of chaos mixed with a cheer,
Sweet nectar drips, drawing us near.

So let's savor every silly scoop,
Together we bathe in this frothy loop.
In a world of flavors, we take the lead,
In sweet serendipity, love takes heed.

Threads of Longing Weaved

We play with yarn, as kittens might,
Tangles and knots in warm twilight.
With every stitch, a giggle hides,
Creating dreams where happiness abides.

Colors collide in a vibrant swirl,
Crafting a blanket, a cozy girl.
Every thread tells a quirky tale,
Stitching our whims in detail.

A tug here, a pull there, the fabric bends,
With laughter stitched tight, our fun never ends.
Snuggled together, our hearts entwined,
In the seams of joy, true love we find.

So let's keep weaving our silly delight,
Creating a tapestry that feels just right.
With every knot, a memory spun,
In threads of longing, our hearts have won.

Surrendering to the Tang of Eden

In gardens where the fruits grow bold,
A pear wore glasses, looking quite old.
He said to the peach, with a wink and a grin,
"Let's tango in syrup and see who'll win!"

The apple chimed in, with a sassy retort,
"I'm the star here, it's quite the sport!"
A melon rolled by, laughing out loud,
"Join me in juice, it's a juicy crowd!"

Siren Songs in Ripened Fields

The corn sings sweetly, like a love-struck fool,
While pumpkins all jest, trying to look cool.
The squash serenades with a crook in its vine,
"Come dance in the twilight, it's going to be fine!"

Oh, carrots chime in, with crunch in their cheer,
"We'll shimmy and shake, bring your friends over here!"
And all of the herbs join in on the fun,
While the crows just complain, 'we're not done!'

Tantalizing Hues of Want

A cherry blushed bright, its cheeks full of glee,
"I'm the center of pie, come capture me!"
Blueberries laughed, with a hearty delight,
"We'll roll in the sunshine, let's party all night!"

The grapes formed a club, wearing hats made of vine,
"Our hangout's the best, and oh so divine!"
A fruit punch approached, stirred with flair,
"Join me for fun; I'm the life of the fair!"

Lurking in the Glade of Yearning

In secret, the berries made plans for a spree,
While cucumbers plotted, all sneaky yet free.
With whispers of love, they danced in the night,
"Who knew that fresh veggies could feel so right?"

Amid the lush greens, there's laughter galore,
As peas in their pods keep asking for more.
"Let's throw a bash, with dips and some chips,
And savor each moment, with zest on our lips!"

Raw and Unfiltered Longing

In the fridge, a cake so bold,
Its frosting whispers secrets told.
I dive right in, no fork in sight,
My cravings dance, a sweet delight.

The clock strikes twelve, my stomach growls,
A midnight snack, oh how it prowls.
I make a mess, icing in my hair,
While dreams of snacks float everywhere.

With cookies calling, I start to drool,
My willpower drops, I play the fool.
A hoard of treats, my heart's on fire,
Who knew I'd be such a snacking liar?

So here I lie, in chocolate bliss,
Regrets are few, I take a risk.
In this sweet chaos, I truly bask,
Finding joy in wishful snack attacks.

Embracing the Undesired

I fancy a fruit that's far too ripe,
But all that's left is a furry type.
I take a bite, the juice does squirt,
And now my shirt's a work of dirt.

The craft beer I crave, hard and extreme,
Turns out a soda's my only dream.
With bubbles rising, I toast to fate,
Who knew my taste would oscillate?

A soggy sandwich—I take a chance,
With pickles on top, I'm in a trance.
A culinary mess, it's pretty clear,
Dinner is served, but I shed a tear.

Yet here I stand, with grin and glee,
A culinary artist, let's wait and see.
For all that's weird and not so grand,
I'll take it all, it's just my brand.

The Lure of the Unattainable

A golden burger glowing bright,
Yet from my reach, it takes its flight.
I chase it round, it runs so fast,
My hopes dashed, yet I'm still cast.

At every corner, a menu tease,
With offer'd pies, oh such sweet ease.
But there it goes, beyond the glass,
A moment's bliss that should not pass.

I spot a pizza, perfectly round,
But upon my plate, just crumbs are found.
Each cheesy dream slips through my grasp,
I'm left with nothing but a wistful gasp.

But in this quest for snacks divine,
I laugh instead of toe the line.
For every bite that's out of reach,
At least this tale is fun to preach.

Shadows of Unquenched Thirst

A jug of lemonade sits on the shelf,
Yet I pour myself a drink from the elf.
With fizz so strong, I feel the burn,
This thirst of mine, it'll take a turn.

With sips of coffee that taste like mud,
I dream of silk, I crave the flood.
But here I stand, my dreams at bay,
With awkward grins, I'll save the day.

A smoothie beckons, all colorful and bright,
But with half an avocado, it's quite the plight.
I gulp it down, no shame in sight,
For even bad drinks can bring delight.

So here's to longing, that funny chase,
Where every sip finds a unique place.
In laughter's arms, I find my cheer,
A toast to thirst, my dear, oh dear!

The Pulse of Yearning Hearts

In the market of longing, we trade sweet smiles,
With prices marked high, but we bargain for miles.
A wink here, a nudge there, like a game of charades,
As we shuffle our hearts in the oddest parades.

The clock chimes so loud, like a comical scene,
We giggle and blush, pretending we're keen.
With stumbles and trips on this path made of glee,
Our wallets may empty, but our spirits are free.

Like puppies in love, we chase after dreams,
In a world silly sweet, bursting at the seams.
With funny little phrases that don't make much sense,
We're masters of laughter, thickening the suspense.

When the yearning's a dance, oh how we spin,
With two left feet in this game called "let's win."
And who cares if we trip, or if we collide?
It's all in good fun, joy our only guide.

Twirling in Desire's Dance

With spins and twirls, we waltz through the night,
Chasing after giggles like they're fireflies bright.
Lost in a whirlpool of whimsical thoughts,
Twirling and skipping, in a dance that begot.

Each step like a puzzle, a jigsaw of laughs,
We trip on our dreams, take our own silly paths.
With grins plastered wide, we fumble and slide,
In a masquerade where our secrets can't hide.

The music's alive with a jazzy refrain,
While our hearts do the cha-cha and feel no pain.
Each glance that we steal feels like a wild chance,
As we glide ever closer, entranced in this dance.

In this comedy show, with hearts all aglow,
We're actors and dancers in a hilarious flow.
So let's swirl on this stage, let the laughter ignite,
For it's fun in the moonlight, in our own silly flight.

Untamed Echoes of Want

In the echoing halls of playful desire,
We tumble and tumble, not wanting to tire.
With whispers of laughter and promises bold,
We chase every flicker, if fortune be sold.

The voices of want, like a mischievous tune,
Make us leap through the air, under the moon.
With a wink and a nod, we dodge and we play,
A game of best hopes on this funny ballet.

Our hearts beat in rhythm, a raucous delight,
As we giggle and spring in the shimmering light.
Each flutter a dare, a game without rules,
In the land of "what if," we dance like sweet fools.

So let's croon to the night, with our hearts all ablaze,
Echoing laughter, in the silliest ways.
For if want is untamed, then let it take flight,
As we tickle the stars in our whimsical night.

Gardens of Lingering Glances

In the garden of glances, where laughter does bloom,
We chase after daisies, dispelling the gloom.
With petals of charm that flutter and flit,
We play hide and seek, not wanting to quit.

Each gaze is a seed, planted right in our souls,
Creating a patchwork of whimsical goals.
With winks that are cheeky and smiles that are bright,
We're cultivating dreams under soft starlight.

Through the thorns and the blossoms, we waltz with delight,
In this comical field, where romance takes flight.
Giggles sprout wildly, like fluffy white clouds,
In a hilarious hedge, our hearts dance unbowed.

So let's roam this garden, where dreams intertwine,
With a bouquet of joy, so playful, divine.
Hand in hand through the rows, we'll savor each part,
For the blooms of affection are sewn in the heart.

The Veil of Soft Sighs

In the garden where whispers play,
Laughter dances, come what may.
With every petal that drops to the ground,
A giggle escapes, a joy so profound.

Beneath the trees where shadows peek,
A squirrel winks, as though to speak.
Grab a snack, take a seat on the grass,
In this silly scene, how the moments amass.

The breeze tickles, the fruits sway low,
The sun's a jokester, setting the show.
In this playful world of colors so bright,
Every soft sigh is a giggle of light.

So join the game, let your heart take flight,
Amongst the laughter, everything feels right.
With a wink and a smile, we dare to explore,
In the veil of soft sighs, who could ask for more?

Save me a Seat Among the Orchards

In orchards where secrets tenderly bloom,
I'll save you a seat amid the perfume.
The apples are blushing, pears laugh aloud,
Under the sun, we'll make our own crowd.

Plucking stars from the sky, they promise delight,
While bees do the tango, from morning till night.
The chirps of the birds, like gossip unfurl,
As they spill all the tea on the world and its swirl.

With cider that sparkles, let's share all our dreams,
Like sticky sweet honey, life's better in teams.
A picnic blanket sprawled, a feast on display,
Every bite a giggle, let's savor the play.

So save me a seat, my friend, do not fret,
Amongst these fine fruits, we'll laugh without debt.
In the orchard of laughter, where joy is the key,
We'll plant seeds of humor, just you and me.

Elixirs of Awakening Dreams.

In a cauldron of whimsy, let's brew up some fun,
With giggles and snickers, our potion's begun.
A dash of wild wishes, a pinch of pure night,
Stirred with mischief until it feels right.

The corks pop like laughter, the bubbles do sing,
As dandelion wishes take off on the wing.
Sipping our elixirs, we'll dance with the breeze,
In this world of enchantment, our hearts are at ease.

With each playful swig, let's awaken the dreams,
Chasing clouds of delight through the wild, wacky schemes.
A feast of the fanciful, where giggles abound,
In the elixirs of laughter, new happiness found.

So pour another round, let the merriment flow,
In this whimsical realm, there's nowhere to go.
With a toast to the silliness, our hearts take flight,
In elixirs of dreams, life sparkles so bright.

Fruits of Forbidden Longing

In a garden of secrets, where shadows tease light,
The fruits hang like whispers, a delicious delight.
With a giggle and smirk, I reach for the treat,
But the branches chuckle, can't quite take a seat.

Oh, the grapes gossip sweetly, with stories to share,
While cherries throw winks, as they tumble through air.
Each berry a promise, wild and unkempt,
In this quirky arena, rules are exempt.

Stumbling over laughter, I trip on a vine,
With each fruity crush, I just can't help but grin.
These luscious temptations invite me to play,
In the orchard of longing where giggles hold sway.

So let's dance with the apples, embrace every whim,
In fruits of desire, our chances aren't slim.
With every delicious bite, let's savor the thrill,
In this playful paradise, our wishes fulfill.

Juices of Longing

In the orchard, I spy, oh my,
A peach wearing a cheeky grin,
It whispers sweet secrets to me,
With every bite, the fun begins.

Cherries giggle on the vine,
Winking at me with their bling,
When I reach for that juicy line,
It's like they're doing a spring fling.

Plums parade in purple delight,
Taunting me with their luscious glow,
I nibble just one, and oh, what a sight,
Suddenly, my heart's all aglow.

This harvest makes me crave the day,
When fruits throw a wild dance party,
With juices flowing, come what may,
I laugh and eat—oh, what a hearty!

Forbidden Fruit's Kiss

Under the moon, the apples gleam,
A secretive glance, oh, what a tease,
Biting into dreams, like a wild dream,
Those crunchy spirits put me at ease.

Pineapples don their party hats,
Dancing with laughter in the breeze,
Kiwi conspiracies in the chats,
Making my heart jump like it's on keys.

Oranges roll like a silly ball,
Citrus cheerleaders in a row,
With each squirt, I stumble and fall,
Forgetting my worries in the show.

Come join the fruit fiesta near,
Where every pout is just a tease,
We sip on pleasure, filled with cheer,
Giggling with flavors, oh what a breeze!

Harvest of Yearning

Fall brings a treasure to my door,
Pumpkins wink with a cheeky stare,
I carve out giggles, who could want more?
The harvest dances, light as air.

Corn on the cob does a silly jig,
Popping kernels like confetti burst,
In a buttery swirl, the flavors dig,
My festive cravings, oh how they thirst!

Carrots wear shades, they look so cool,
Basking in sun, they laugh all day,
I munch on greens, feeling like a fool,
As the veggie party carries me away.

With every bite, I break into song,
This harvest of joy is never wrong,
So grab a seat, come join along,
In the garden of dreams where we all belong!

Cravings Beneath the Blossoms

Beneath the blossoms, sweet scents collide,
Bees buzz softly, oh what a scene,
I chase the nectar with joy and pride,
Turning each blossom into a dream.

Lavender winks with a fragrant flair,
As I dive in for a cheeky sip,
Rose petals fall like love in the air,
I almost forgot my planned fruit trip.

Lilies giggle, making wishes fly,
While daffodils dance in the sun,
With petals plucked, I reach for the sky,
These cravings blossom, oh what fun!

To play among the petals, so bright,
Is to feast on laughter and pure delight,
Here in the blooms, everything's right,
My heart's a garden and takes flight!

Sated in the Shadows

In the dim light, they plot their schemes,
With giggles and whispers, weaving their dreams.
An apple in hand, a wink in the air,
The night holds secrets, no reason to care.

They dance like shadows on walls that conform,
With clumsy steps, their laughter a storm.
Who knew romance could be such a riot?
Like cats in a hat, they just can't be quiet.

Mismatched socks and a roast burned black,
"This isn't love," one said, "it's a snack!"
An awkward embrace, a popcorn fight,
As passion brews in the soft moonlight.

At dawn they'll chuckle, all red-faced and bright,
Recalling the mischief from their wild night.
In the shadows they thrived, so playful, so spry,
With hearts full of laughter, they reached for the sky.

Seduction at Sundown

As the sun dips low and the sky turns to gold,
Two hearts collide; they're feeling quite bold.
With glances and snacks, they plot out their play,
This date is a game, like a kid's cabaret.

A flick of the wrist, a noodle is tossed,
"Wait, did you catch that?" "Nope, I was lost!"
They mock and they fumble, it's all part of the charm,
With each little blunder, they sound the alarm.

Sundown allure, oh such silly flings,
She holds him close, while he finds her wings.
"Don't pluck my petals!" she giggles and sways,
As the sun bids goodbye and the stars dance and play.

With ice cream in hand, they lean down to sip,
And bellyache laughter turns into a trip.
At twilight they'll ponder, with wide grins and sighs,
How silly love dances under silly skies.

Tangled Vines of Passion

In a garden wild where the weeds grow thick,
Two hearts find roots, though it's quite a trick.
They trip over flowers, all tangled and torn,
"Is this love," she asks, "or just a bad thorn?"

They pull at the vines with a fervor so grand,
But the more that they tug, the more they withstand.
A kiss in the chaos, a giggle ensues,
As honeybees buzz, oh they can't help but snooze.

Around each other like vines they twist,
Mirth in each rustle, it's too good to miss.
"Let's plant our own seeds, if you're up for the mess,"
But first, she retorts, "Let's not forget the dress!"

With dirt on their shoes and crumbs on their lips,
A duo of joy, here come the funny slips.
In this garden of whimsy, their laughter ignites,
A salad of passion that simply delights.

Open Heart Orchard

In an orchard of whimsy, where fruit flies delight,
They share tales of nonsense as day turns to night.
An orange is tossed like a ball of sweet jest,
And laughter erupts, like a fruit salad fest.

He leans on a tree, with a grin that won't stop,
"Is it love or just apples?" She giggles, "A flop!"
With each silly question, more giggles take flight,
In the branches above, they chuckle with might.

She plucks at the petals, mischief in bloom,
"Can we carve our initials? Let's make room for doom!"
A squirrel joins in, with his own playful scheme,
As their laughter ripples like a carefree dream.

In this orchard of tales, where sweetness abounds,
They count all the giggles, no need for new bounds.
With every bright sunset, their hearts thrice entwine,
In a world full of whimsy, they toast with sweet wine.

Glimmers of a Yearned Touch

In the kitchen, pots go clang,
Love's recipe, it's quite the bang.
Sugar and spice, a pinch of tease,
Whisk it all until you freeze.

Muffin tops and wobbly pies,
A culinary dream, oh how it flies!
Spatula battle with flour in the air,
I bake my heart, do you dare to share?

Mixing sweetness in a bowl,
Desserts or love, I can't control.
You're the cherry on my cake,
Let's spoon together, for goodness' sake!

Flour dust dances in the light,
Do I smell romance or a cake fight?
Frosting lips and sugar rush,
Let's indulge in this playful hush!

The Heart's Private Sanctuary

In my closet, secrets hide,
A treasure chest, my heart's pride.
Love notes scribbled on old shoes,
Wearing feelings, what do I choose?

Napping softly on the bed,
Dreams of you swirl in my head.
I bought a teddy, it looks quite shy,
Cuddly chums, who can deny?

Pillow fort of emotions grand,
Decorated with hearts, a lovey band.
Tossing whispers to the moon,
In this hideout, I swoon too soon.

Painting hopes on the wall,
My heart sings, can you hear its call?
A sanctuary in playful disguise,
Where love's giggles meet the sighs!

Shadows of Sugar-coated Fantasies

In the candy shop, I lost my wish,
Sweet tooth whispers, I've found my dish.
Chocolate rivers and gummy bears,
A sticky situation, but who really cares?

Lollipop dreams on a sugar high,
Dancing on clouds, oh my, oh my!
Cotton candy clouds puffed so bright,
In this sweet land, everything's right.

Marshmallow fields, a fluffy delight,
Building castles in the moonlight.
Fruity flavors swirl and twist,
In this sweet scene, you can't resist.

Nibbles and giggles all around,
With every crunch, my heart is found.
Sugar-coated dreams, we laugh and play,
In these sweet shadows, we'll stay all day!

Hushed Conversations in the Vineyard

In the vineyard, whispers flow,
Grapes are laughing, don't you know?
Hiding secrets behind the leaves,
Sipping dreams from nature's cleaves.

Under the sun, we toast our cheer,
Plucking fruit with no fear near.
Juicy tales spin in the breeze,
Each grape holds laughter with sweet tease.

With every sip, we giggle and sway,
Spilling stories in a playful way.
Barefoot dancing on earth so fine,
In this grape escape, we intertwine.

Beneath the moon, with fireflies bright,
We chat and chuckle, oh what a sight!
In the vineyard's heart, our joy's alive,
With hushed laughter, our spirits thrive!

The Allure of Midnight Blooms

Under the moon, secrets spin,
Bumbles and giggles, let's begin.
Petals whisper, hear them talk,
Dancing shadows, midnight walk.

A scent so sweet, can't get enough,
Catch me if you can, this stuff!
Bees at play, swirling 'round,
In this garden, joy is found.

Laughter blooms, with every tease,
Frolicking friends, swinging trees.
But watch your step, oh what a fright,
Tripping over flowers at night!

So here we twirl, no care in sight,
Chasing blooms till morning light.
With every giggle, life's a churn,
In midnight's grip, we bask and learn.

Bounty of the Heart

Hearts a-flutter, like a kite,
Could I share this berry bite?
Juicy giggles, sticky hands,
Love's a mess—oh, how it stands!

Cherries burst with a zesty pop,
Each taste leads us to the top.
Yummy, sweet, like warm delight,
Next round's on me, take a bite!

Sunshine smiles, oh what a thrill,
Run to the patch, catch that chill.
With baskets full, we chase our fate,
Squeezing fruit, oh, isn't it great?

Laughter echoes, as we feast,
Friendship grows, hearts never cease.
In this banquet, joy's the start,
Feasting together, bounty of the heart!

Secrets in the Garden

Whispers weaving through the leaves,
Frog on a log, what he believes.
Under each petal, stories bloom,
Making jokes in the earthy gloom.

Pumpkins chuckle, carrots laugh,
As beetroot shows its stylish staff.
Tomatoes blush, red as can be,
What a party, come join me!

Gnomes gossip while flowers sway,
Sharing secrets, come what may.
In this patch of mischief bright,
Sun-kissed dreams take off in flight.

Chickens cluck with vibrant flair,
Chasing worms without a care.
In the garden, life's a play,
Where laughter leads the light of day.

Sap of Eager Hearts

Sappy tales from trees so wise,
Drip, drop, laughter fills the skies.
Maple hugs, syrupy sweet,
Let's dance 'round, and lose our feet!

Under bark, secrets collide,
Squirrels giggle, joining the ride.
Nutty chirps and playful leaps,
In this forest, joy never sleeps.

Honeyed dreams, sticky and bright,
Golden glimmers, oh what a sight!
We share our hopes, take a chance,
In nature's ball, we twirl and prance.

Life is sweet, like syrup poured,
With every laugh, we are adored.
Join the fun, embrace the cheer,
With eager hearts, we persevere.

Hues of Enchantment in Light

In a garden bright with tales to tell,
The daisies wink, casting a spell.
A bumblebee buzzes, quite a flirt,
Chased by a butterfly, dressed in a skirt.

Sunbeams dance, they twirl and sway,
As grasshoppers hop in a playful ballet.
A squirrel steals snacks, quite the sneaky thief,
While flowers gossip, sharing their belief.

A painter dabs colors on a whim,
His canvas filled with a charming grin.
Laughter swirls like candy in the air,
As shadows stretch, drawing our stare.

With every hue, a chuckle is brewed,
In the warm embrace, joy is renewed.
Amidst this riot of laughter and cheer,
Life takes a sip, toasting the year.

The Allure of Lingering Moments

A cookie crumbles, oh so bold,
While whispers of frosting make stories unfold.
Coffee cups clink, just like hearts,
In this warm café, where silliness starts.

Friends juggle donuts, it's quite the show,
One lands on a head, oh no, oh no!
With giggles and snorts, the room comes alive,
Creating new memories, watch them thrive.

The waiter is tripped by a flapjack flap,
And laughter erupts, a delightful mishap.
A spoon takes a dive, splashing tea,
What a fine mess, happy as can be!

In every moment, a hiccup of fun,
Linking hearts under the shimmering sun.
Here's to the magic that keeps us all close,
Where sweet little blunders mean the most.

Revelations in the Garden's Glow

In twilight's embrace, the flowers confide,
About secret crushes and blooms-wide-eyed.
A snail makes a move, reaching for a kiss,
Only to slip, oh what a miss!

Veggies debate, who's the fairest of all,
While radishes blush, and tomatoes enthrall.
Carrots in costumes perform a grand play,
As the moon beams down, lighting their way.

A frog in a crown sings a quirky tune,
Bouncing along under the laughing moon.
The hedgehog giggles, the butterfly flirts,
In this whimsical world, we're all in our shirts.

Under twinkling stars, mischief resumes,
New tales gather as the garden blooms.
With every chuckle, a secret unfolds,
In this patch of delight, where laughter's pure gold.

Spirited Whispers Beneath the Stars

Beneath twinkling skies, the owls start to chat,
Exchanging wisecracks, how's that for a spat?
A raccoon in a hat, so dapper and fine,
Turns to the moon and offers a line.

Fireflies flicker, playing hide and seek,
While crickets compose a melody so chic.
A rabbit in shades gives a wink and a nod,
To the stars above—oh, how they applaud!

The breeze carries laughter with a gentle tease,
As shadows grow longer, dancing with ease.
Laughter of night evokes fun and delight,
In this playful realm where dreams take flight.

With each twinkle and giggle, the night spins anew,
Turning over secrets, just between me and you.
Beneath starlit covers, our stories entwine,
In this raucous embrace, everything feels divine.

Tales of Carnal Kinship

In the kitchen, secrets stir,
While pots gossip, ain't that absurd?
The spices dance, they twist and twirl,
As we plot our culinary whirl.

With butter's charm, we did conspire,
To bake a cake that should inspire.
But flour flew, oh such a mess,
Our sweet affair, a trial, no less!

Turning dough with hopeful dreams,
Flavored kisses and whipped cream screams.
But who's to bake, and who to taste?
A bake-off war, we're both so graced!

In every bite, a love lace spun,
Together we laugh, we're having fun.
With burnt edges and frosting plight,
In our kitchen, the stars ignite.

Lattes and Lasting Glances

At the café, hearts collide,
With frothy mugs, we sip beside.
Your hazel eyes, a puzzling maze,
As mocha drips, the laughter plays.

I spill the cream, oh what a sight,
You giggle soft, my heart takes flight.
With every sip, the tension grows,
A latte love in this warm glow.

Your smile froths, like whipped-up brew,
I try my best to keep it cool.
But things get steamy, oh how they do,
Over coffee grounds, we brew our stew.

So let us sip and share some dreams,
In caffeinated, playful schemes.
For in this café, where beans are tossed,
We'll find the line between joy and frost.

Dreamscapes of Unfulfilled Wishes

In slumber's grasp, we chase the stars,
With wild ideas, and very few bars.
A sky of schemes, balloons that fly,
But dreams can pop, oh me, oh my!

You wished for gold, I wanted fame,
But here we are, both hunting shame.
With zeppelins drifting, hopes anew,
We blend our dreams, a quirky brew.

But in this haze of comic plight,
We laugh at dreams that took to flight.
For every wish, a fits and starts,
A tapestry of tangled hearts.

Oh, what a mess our wishes make,
A grand parade, a wobbly shake.
But in this chaos, one thing's clear,
Together we dance, embracing the cheer.

Entwined in the Evening Mist

In twilight's glow, we weave our fun,
Two shadows joining, but who's the one?
With whispered words, and playful glee,
We lose ourselves, just you and me.

Through evening mist, our laughter flows,
Like giggling ghosts, everyone knows.
With every step, our stories blend,
In this maze, we pretend, pretend!

But tangled up in silly lines,
We trip through stories that fate designs.
Stumbling forth, we find our pace,
A comical chase in this wild space.

So here's to fog and fumbled charms,
To missteps made and open arms.
As night enfolds, our hearts take flight,
Entwined we dance, a funny sight.

Fevered Dreams by Candlelight

The candle flickers low, what a sight,
A dance of shadows, oh what a night!
Whispers of secrets bounce off the walls,
While the cat judges me—what a ball!

I toss and turn in my little bed,
Thoughts of chocolate, and crumbs to spread!
Cakes and pies dance in my mind's parade,
Is it too late for laughs, or sweets homemade?

With every laugh, the flame gets stout,
"What's that?" I mumble, as I curl about.
In fevered dreams, my thoughts ignite,
Are these cravings wrong, or just out of sight?

But in the morning, as daylight beams,
I wake up laughing at my wild schemes.
When dreams collide with a breakfast spree,
Every bite's a wonder, just wait and see!

Cascades of Hidden Intent

At the café, I spot a cute grin,
Coffee spills, oh what a sin!
I ponder deeply, what's the game?
Is he just nice, or does he feel the same?

He stirs his cup like a magic spell,
With every sip, my heart does swell.
Muffin crumbs fall down like rain,
Had I known love had this level of pain?

I sidle close while my heart does flip,
Tripping on thoughts, I take a sip.
His laughter bubbles like soda pop,
But will he really take the leap, or just stop?

In cascades of wishes, our hopes align,
We giggle together, sipping on lime.
But in this dance, let's keep it bright,
Oh, the joy of flirting feels just right!

A Symphony of Blushing Roses

Roses red, violets blue,
I bought some flowers, who knew?
With each petal that I hold,
A secret story starts to unfold.

In my garden, bees hum a tune,
While I dare to daydream under the moon.
"More sugar needed!" I call to the skies,
Hoping my crush realizes, who sighs?

In the bouquet, hidden notes of wit,
With every smile, I'm falling a bit.
But do they know how sweet love can be?
When roses blush, oh can't you see?

So here's to laughter and petals near,
Each moment together, I hold dear.
In this symphony of quirky charms,
Let's dance through life, wrapped in warm arms!

Serpentine Paths of Attraction

Life's a maze, twist and turn,
In every corner, feelings burn.
A chance encounter at the ice cream stand,
With every scoop, I plot my plan.

He drops a cone, oh what a sight!
Laughing together, everything's light.
We swap our flavors, a daring feat,
Connecting over snacks, oh how sweet!

With each step, my heart does race,
Navigating paths, a madcap chase.
Yet those giggles spark a gentle thrill,
In this winding maze, love's a skill.

So here I stand, with a cherry on top,
As we play this game, we can't stop.
Serpentine ways lead to delight,
In clumsy love, everything feels right!

Harvest of Hidden Passions

In the garden where secrets grow,
Tomatoes blush, with tales to show.
A cucumber dances, oh what a spree,
While carrots giggle, 'Come dance with me!'

Bees are buzzing, what do they know?
They're gossiping sweetly, in sun's warm glow.
With veggies wearing their finest attire,
Oh, the laughter in this fragrant choir!

Pickles and peppers have stories to share,
As zucchini plots with flair and dare.
Every vine whispers, with cheeky delight,
In this harvest party, the mood is just right!

So gather your friends, let the feast begin,
With salads so funny, we'll surely win.
We'll toast to the joy, from the top of our heads,
In this garden of giggles, where no one dreads.

Whispers Beneath the Bloom

Under petals soft, where whispers play,
Lilies chuckle at the bees' ballet.
A rose winks slyly, with petals so bold,
While daisies nod, their secrets unfold.

Beneath the blossoms, laughter runs free,
Tulips are plotting botanical glee.
With sunshine spilling, the daisies conspire,
To spread rumors of love, or maybe just fire!

In this floral circus, scents intertwine,
As poppies blush crimson, with humor divine.
Oh, what a riot, this garden's so sly,
With bees buzzing secrets and butterflies shy!

As petals unfold, and taunts take their flight,
The blooms hold their breath, waiting for night.
With laughter and whimsy, the blooms intertwine,
In this fragrant farce, everything's fine!

Temptation's Juicy Secrets

In orchards where flavors flirt and tease,
The apples giggle, rustling the leaves.
Peaches blush crimson, just hanging around,
While grapefruits yap, the juiciest sound!

Oh, strawberry whispers, with mischief in mind,
"Let's throw a party, leave worries behind!"
With a lemon twist, the punch bowl stands tall,
While cherries chuckle, they'll catch us all!

Plum joke-tellers share tales fruity and sweet,
While oranges balance, no sign of defeat.
Every fruit in the basket knows how to jest,
In this luscious kingdom, they're simply the best!

As fruit flies spin tales, the laughter erupts,
While nibbled delights leave us feeling pumped.
Join the temptation, let the fun descend,
In this juicy adventure, where giggles don't end!

Lush Dreams Entwined

In dreams so lush, where giggles bloom,
Berries pile high, dispelling our gloom.
Cucumbers wrestle, with glee in their eyes,
While snap peas cheer, filled with surprise!

A banquet of laughter, bright and so bold,
Carrots tell tales that never grow old.
In veggie attire, they cast aside fears,
With laughter as spice, and no room for tears!

Tomatoes are blending, their shades on parade,
While squash plays the fool, with jokes that don't fade.
Oh, harvest your smiles, let them intertwine,
In this comical garden, everything's fine!

So gather your friends, let the feasting abound,
With belly laughs ringing, a joyous sound.
In lush dreams together, our spirits will climb,
With fruits of our laughter, we'll savor the rhyme!

When Yearning Meets Abundance

In the fridge, leftovers pile,
Yet I'm craving gourmet style.
A pickle's waltz, a jelly dance,
My taste buds scream, give me a chance!

Cupcakes call with their frosted grace,
I chase them down; oh, what a race!
A doughnut spins, with doughnut zeal,
But salad whispers, 'Let's keep it real.'

The pantry's packed, yet still I pine,
For snacks unmade, oh how divine!
I vow to bake, with sweet delight,
Yet kitchen chaos keeps me up at night!

A fruit parade on my dining plate,
That apple's cute, but there's cake to sate.
With every bite, my heart's aglow,
As cravings dance, a comedy show!

Luscious Echoes of the Heart

In a bakery, sweet whispers fly,
Cookies giggle as I walk by.
The scones strut in powdered coats,
While muffins wear their nutty quotes.

Dough rising high, like dreams on air,
Pies wink at me with fruity flair.
Each layer calls, a sugary tease,
Like my resolve—crumbles with ease!

Chocolate fountains like rivers flow,
I dive right in, the world a show.
Donuts gleam with sprinkles bright,
While cupcakes wink in morning light.

With every bite, I soar and sway,
Desires dance in a playful way.
Like giggly friends at a wild party,
Each scrumptious morsel, oh so hearty!

The Sweetness of Daring Dreams

A candy land where wishes grow,
Every treat sings, 'Just take it slow!'
Gummy bears wearing party hats,
Share secrets sweet from tiny chats.

The ice cream truck's a siren's song,
Chasing it feels so delightfully wrong.
A spritz of fudge, a whirl of cream,
Daring dreams wrapped in a sugary dream!

Cotton candy clouds float through the air,
I reach to pluck, but there's none to share.
Jelly beans in every hue,
In this candy realm, I'm never blue!

Each sugar rush ignites my soul,
As lollipops play their sugary role.
A taste of daring, light and bright,
Oh, sweet adventure in every bite!

Blossoms of Longing's Embrace

In the garden, cupcakes bloom,
Frosting petals fill the room.
Each one whispers, 'Take a taste!'
While I wonder how many, in haste?

A chocolate fountain flows with flair,
Dipped strawberries without a care.
I'm planting seeds of sugary cheer,
As cookie critters gather near!

With every bloom, my heart takes flight,
Marshmallow clouds, fluffy and white.
They giggle as I reach with glee,
'Come join the fun, just taste with me!'

The pie tree sways, a tempting sight,
While brownies wink in the soft moonlight.
In a world of bake-off dreams and fame,
Each scrumptious wish, a playful game!

Embracing the Forbidden

In shadows we giggle, the clock strikes eleven,
A cookie jar stolen, a slice from heaven.
Two spoons in one bowl, still fighting the spoon,
Caution's a joke when laughing's in bloom.

The thrill of the chase, a flirt with the cake,
"Just one more bite" we whisper, half-fake.
With frosting on noses, we dance to the beat,
Sharing our secrets, the laughter so sweet.

A glance at the fridge, eyes wide, what a sight!
Ketchup and ice cream, who knew it felt right?
With sprinkles and giggles, we toast to the night,
Two bizarre chefs, oh, what pure delight!

The clock ticking down, our stash running dry,
"Hurry!" we shout, as we laugh and we sigh.
Forbidden delights, in this kitchen we're kings,
With frosting and friendship, oh, sweet little things!

The Ritual of Unveiling

In fancy attire, we gather around,
With cake on our faces, we know we've found.
Giggling and winking, the forks at the ready,
A feast for the senses, oh, hold your confetti!

The curtains are drawn, here comes the surprise,
A banana in pajamas? Oh, what a guise!
With laughter and cheer, we unveil our stash,
A table of treats, it's a sugary bash!

Among the delights, a piñata so bright,
Filled with revolting candy, oh what a sight!
As we swing and we miss, the hilarity grows,
Chocolate and chaos, and confetti bestows.

At the end of our feast, with crumbs on the floor,
We dance in our sugar high, wanting more.
Embracing the silly, with joy we unveil,
The laughter we share, it will always prevail!

An Abundance of Sweet Affection

With jellybean flowers, and candy cane trees,
We frolic through fields, our love's just a tease.
Cuddling up close with our licorice friends,
In sugar-coated dreams, the fun never ends.

Chocolate chip rain falls, we skip and we play,
Creating a world where gumdrops sway.
With each little giggle, we feast on delight,
Sprinkling our laughter from morning till night.

A dance in the rain with a frosting embrace,
Two silly souls lost in jubilant space.
Floating on marshmallows, riding on bliss,
We twirl through the sweetness, with each goofy kiss.

In this sugary land where our hearts intertwine,
The sweetness of us, oh, how perfectly fine!
With a wink and a grin, the affection we share,
Is a bubble of sweetness beyond all compare!

Gentle Temptations of the Night

Under the moonlight, we plot and we scheme,
With cookies and giggles, we're living the dream.
A sprinkle or two, oh, what mischief we make,
As stars wink above, we dive into cake.

The night is our canvas, frosted with fun,
With laughter and whispers, until we are done.
Each slice, sweet and sticky, brings joy to the plate,
In this whimsical realm, we dance with fate.

With silhouettes darting and giggles that flit,
The mischief is brewing, oh, isn't it lit?
With each little nibble, our hearts intertwined,
In the garden of laughter, no rules are defined.

As dawn peeks through curtains, we whisper and sigh,
Our secrets and sweets, beneath the sky high.
Embracing the warmth of our midnight delight,
With chocolatey smiles, we bid farewell to the night!

Autumn's Lure

Leaves dance down with capricious flair,
Squirrels flirt, not a single care.
Pumpkin spice wafts through the crisp air,
While I try to act like I'm unaware.

Cider's bubbling, oh what a sight,
Yet somehow it's turned into a fight.
We chase each other in costumes so tight,
As pumpkins giggle in the fading light.

The Weight of Unsung Affection

In the corner, he stands with a frown,
A lingering look, not quite a clown.
While hearts play tag and hopes tumble down,
His sandwich is left stone-cold and brown.

With each awkward word, a giggle erupts,
As the whole group giggles, and then erupts.
A love note scribbled, but never picked up,
Like a forgotten cup from the coffee shop.

Garden of the Unattainable

Among the weeds lies a secret wish,
A tomato that dreams of becoming a dish.
The flowers spin tales, their petals all swish,
While bumbles buzz by, with no time to squish.

Bananas are dancing, a tropical scene,
With strawberries plotting a ketchup machine.
Yet here I stand, in this leafy cuisine,
Watching them party, and feeling quite green.

Surrendering to Sweet Chaos

A cake tipped over, frosting like rain,
Still, we all cheer, 'What fun, what a gain!'
Laughter erupts, though some feel the pain,
Of icing that sticks on every last grain.

The sprinkler's on dance floors, we spin, we glide,
As water balloons whisper, 'Come join the ride!'
Each splat a giggle, we've nowhere to hide,
In this sweet chaos, we'll dance side by side.

www.ingramcontent.com/pod-product-compliance
Lightning Source LLC
Chambersburg PA
CBHW060121230426
43661CB00003B/280